More SERMON OUTLINES ON SPECIAL DAYS AND OCCASIONS

Charles R. Wood

KREGEL PUBLICATIONS
Grand Rapids, Michigan 49501

More Sermon Outlines for Special Days and Occasions,
by Charles R. Wood. © 1990 by Kregel Publications, a
division of Kregel, Inc., P. O. Box 2607, Grand Rapids,
MI 49501. All rights reserved.

Cover: Don Ellens

Library of Congress Cataloging-in-Publication Data

More sermon outlines for special days and occasions /
Charles R. Wood.
   p.   cm.—(Easy-to-use sermon outline series)
Includes index.

1. Church year sermons—Outlines, syllabi, etc.
2. Occasional sermons—Outlines, syllabi, etc. I. Title.
II. Series: Wood, Charles R. (Charles Robert), 1933-
Easy-to-use sermon outline series.

BV4223.W66   1990   251'.02—dc20   90-38561
                                                        CIP
ISBN   0-8254-3987-6 (pbk.)

        1 2 3 4 5 Printing/Year 94 93 92 91 90

Printed in the United States of America

Contents

Textual Index

Introduction

Special days and occasions are always taxing from the standpoint of the preacher. Where to find the exact message for the hour becomes a major concern, and many who might not normally turn to a book of outlines such as this are drawn by the possible solution it offers to their dilemma.

Although not claiming to provide an exhaustive coverage of all the various special occasions one might be called upon to address, an attempt is made at a broad coverage of occasions and an indepth treatment of those that place the greatest demands upon the preacher-speaker.

The Christmas outlines included are unique in that five of the six are based on a single theme and are thus ideal for a series of sermons. Such series treatment is not necessary as each message will stand on its own merits, but the provision of a potential series might be of assistance given the fact that three or four weeks are often devoted to Christmas messages and the preacher is often required to minister to a variety of groups at that sacred season.

Several of the outlines specifically identified with Easter are not limited to that specialized use but are also well suited to other special occasions such as New Year's, a funeral, or even baptismal or communion observances.

The nature of the occasions that prompt these sermons dictates that they not be as uniformly expository as the compiler might normally wish, but an attempt has been made to make them more than superficial subjective treatments.

Time invested in studying the indicated scriptural passage as well as in thoughtfully considering the contents of the outlines themselves will be well rewarded. No one should hesitate to alter any outline to suit his own style of organization and presentation. Many of the messages are susceptible to reorganization and have the potential of suggesting another train of thought which might lead to one or more additional messages arising from a single outline.

All of the messages have been born in the crucible of prayer and study. They have been sharpened through the process of preaching and further honed for publication. Hopefully, they are "preachable" and will ideally provide the need for that special message for a special time.

The God of New Beginnings

Genesis 35

Introduction

This is the time of year when we stress the chance to start over again. Almost every one has wished he could start over at one time or another. It is interesting to note that many men in the Bible were given new beginnings in life.

I. **Men Who Had New Beginnings**
  A. Abraham
   1. Man of unknown obscurity in Ur of the Chaldees.
   2. Rose to fantastic prominence as head of a great and immortal nation.
  B. Jacob
   1. Was a man of fleshly ways.
      a. Tricky and self-willed.
      b. Actually bore character description in name.
   2. Became a man of deep spiritual conviction and presence.
  C. Joseph
   1. Oppressed through no fault of his own.
   2. Became a man greatly honored and revered.
  D. Moses
   1. Was involved in an unfortunate incident of self-willed failure in slaying the Egyptian.
   2. Became one of God's most dynamic leaders.
  E. David
   1. Fell from a pinnacle of power into a debacle of degradation.
   2. Was restored to a place of great usefulness.
  F. Peter
   1. Became the classic example of failure through his denial of Christ.
   2. Lived to become one of the pillars of church.
  G. Paul
   1. Wasted his life in opposing Christ and Gospel.
   2. Later became one of most used men of all time.

II. **The Source of New Beginnings**
  A. The place where they started.
   1. Abraham: obscurity.
   2. Jacob: a crafty, self-willed failure.

3. Joseph: an innocent victim of circumstance.
4. Moses: an impatient, un-yielded failure.
5. David: a sinning, morally-corrupt flop.
6. Peter: a Christ denying turn-coat.
7. Paul: a viscious, Christ-battling opponent.
B. The significant mode of change (God intervened in each one of these cases).
C. The varied modes of God's intervention.
   1. Through response to His call: Abraham.
   2. Through over-powering of self-will: Jacob.
   3. Through reversal of circumstances: Joseph.
   4. Through a period of enriching isolation: Moses.
   5. Through a stinging, accusing rebuke: David.
   6. Through a tender session of reapproachment: Peter.
   7. Through a stunning self-revelation of truth: Paul.
D. God worked in a different way in each case, but it was God that effected the change!

III. The Implications of New Beginnings
A. Full range of "before" situations is run (almost everything that might make one want to start over).
   1. Obscurity.
   2. Self-will.
   3. Victimization by circumstances.
   4. Unyieldedness.
   5. Sin and moral failure.
   6. Flat, outright denial.
   7. Rejection of biblical truth.
B. Certain elements common to each (although stories are very dissimilar).
   1. Each was really in a mess (especially spiritually).
   2. Each needed a new beginning.
   3. God gave new beginnings to each.
   4. Each went on to great accomplishments.
C. Certain aspects are pertinent to us.
   1. Any man can have opportunity of starting over.
   2. Only the God-given new beginning offers any guarantee of success.
   3. Somewhere in this must be a willingness to cast ourselves on God and allow Him to make new.

Conclusion
God can give a new beginning. Only He can give one guaranteed to last. Will you call upon Him for that?

A New Year's Resolution for Everyone

John 14:15-24

Introduction

The Lord left a project for all of us to do. He said, "If ye love, keep my commandments," and he then expanded on that statement. What excellent material for a New Year's resolution.

I. **Love and Obedience Go Together (vv. 15, 21, 23)**
   A. Repeated three times.
      1. Verse 15: if you love me, keep my commandments.
      2. Verse 21: if you keep my commandments, you love me—other side of the same statement.
      3. Verse 23: statement personalized—not just a general matter for everyone.
   B. Form two ways of saying the same thing.
      1. If you love me, keep my commandments; if you keep my commandments, you love me.
      2. We can talk of obedient love and of loving obedience.
   C. Main truth: can't part love and obedience when it comes to the Lord.

II. **Obedient Love Is a Very Broad Matter (vv. 21, 23, 24)**
   A. Goes beyond commandments.
      1. Includes commandments, words (v. 23) and sayings (v. 24).
      2. Not adequate to go through and pick out commandments one likes, keep them and then pride self on that performance.
   B. Involves knowing what He wants (v. 24).
      1. Phrase can be turned around.
      2. Real love for Him never pleads ignorance—always seeks to find new ways to please Him by obedience.
   C. Includes all of His word (v. 24b).
      1. What Christ taught was not of Himself.
      2. His teaching was of God—therefore we are under obligation to do all that the Word teaches.

III. **Obedient Love Brings Us Closer to the Lord (vv. 21b, 23b)**
   A. We are loved as a reward for obedience.
      1. He loved us in the first place.
      2. He adds more love to those who are obedient.
   B. We receive a special awareness of His presence as a result of obedience.

1. He manifests Himself in response to obedience.
2. He dwells in a special way with the obedient.

C. The key to the "deeper life" lies in obedience.
1. Deeper life desires to know Him better.
2. This passage says that the way to know Him better is to obey what He says.
3. The Biblical deeper life is a matter of going deeper into His Word and practicing it.

IV. **Obedient Love Only Possible by the Holy Spirit (vv. 16-20)**
A. This explains verses 16-20.
1. Verses are not here by accident.
2. Speak of Holy Spirit right in the context of obedience.
B. Holy Spirit is necessarily involved in obedient love.
1. He recorded the commandments, words, and sayings.
2. He is the one who enables us to obey and live by these things.

V. **Lack of Obedience Is Evidence of Lack of Love (v. 24)**
A. Just as presence of obedience shows presence of love, so lack of obedience shows lack of love.
B. Lack of love shown by lack of obedience may be the result of.
1. Ignorance.
2. Never really having come to know Christ as Savior and Lord.

Conclusion

New Year's resolution for everyone:
- Love the Lord more this year.
- Go deeper with Him by knowing more of what He expects of me.
- Obeying all that I know.

First Things First

Matthew 6:33

Introduction

It is fairly easy to be a good Christian when in church. It is more difficult at places such as the home and at the market place where we earn our wages. God wants us to be Christians everywhere, and good Christians at that. It isn't easy, but He gives us the help that we need if only we will accept what He teaches.

I. **Our Occupation**
   A. There are three key issues in life.
      1. Lodging.
      2. Clothing.
      3. Food.
   B. We spend at least half of our waking hours with involvement in these things.
      1. Probably more concern invested in these than in anything else.
      2. These things loom large in importance.

II. **Our Options**
   A. Verse indicates that there are two options.
      1. We can go after things as our goal.
      2. We can seek the kingdom and righteousness of God as our goal.
   B. We generally do it other than as the verse says.
      1. We go after the material things that loom large in life.
      2. We give small attention to the spiritual things of life (somehow, we expect them to take care of themselves).

III. **Our Objectives**
   A. We can go after "these other things."
      1. Primary concern with housing, food, clothing.
      2. Our goals in the direction of the material.
   B. We can go after the kingdom and righteousness.
      1. Kingdom—that which recognizes and promotes His rule and reign.
      2. Righteousness—that which is in accord with His character.
      3. Summary—the spiritual as opposed to the material.

IV. **Our Order**
   A. What the verse does not teach.

1. It is not wrong to go after other things.
2. We do not have to spend our entire time in spiritual pursuits.
B. What it does teach.
   1. If you are going to be consumed with anything, be consumed with the kingdom.
   2. Clearly establish priorities of life.

V. **Our Obtaining**
   A. There are two ways of getting things.
      1. Struggling for them and making them the object of life.
      2. Having them added unto you.
   B. The way to get the things we usually desire is to make them a matter of lower priority.
      1. This is a promise.
      2. This is a conditional promise.

VI. **Our Operation**
   A. It means that we must not expect His blessing where He is not first.
      1. May explain some unproductive giving.
      2. Comes as a warning—don't expect Him to bless you if you are not going to put Him first.
   B. It means that every decision in life must be weighed.
      1. What am I putting first?
      2. Every decision must give priority to the Lord.
   C. We must give God sovereignty over our lives.
      1. This is where the real issue lies.
      2. This must include the lordship implied in salvation.

Conclusion
Two simple rules should govern life. Set your eyes on the things that advance His kingdom and contribute to the establishment of His righteousness and go after them. Allow the heavenly Father to keep His promises concerning the rest of life.

A Text for Valentine's Day

Proverbs 4:2, 3

Introduction

Hearts are deeply associated with the day, and the Bible has so very much to say about hearts. There is one key passage in Proverbs that provides a splendid consideration at Valentines' Day.

I. **What Are We to Do About the Heart?**
- A. The heart is:
  1. The inner man.
  2. The center of emotions, affections, moral consciousness.
- B. We are to give it special attention.
  1. "Guard it with all guarding."
  2. "Above all other things you guard, guard your heart."

II. **Why Are We to Guard the Heart?**
- A. Because God ponders it (Prov. 21:2; 24:12).
  1. He knows it.
  2. He searches it for motives.
  3. He weighs and evaluates it.
- B. Because it is the starting point of rebellion (Prov. 19:3).
  1. Rebellion never begins with action.
  2. It is always a decision of the will.
- C. Because it is the starting ground of backsliding (Prov. 14:14).
  1. Backsliding always begins and ends in heart.
     - a. Starts with coldness.
     - b. Ends with breaking.
  2. Right heart never backslides.
- D. Because it is the starting point for obedience (Prov. 3:1).
  1. We can keep commandments by simply doing what we are told.
  2. But best to keep from heart.
- E. Because it sets tone of spirit (Prov. 15:13).
  1. Heart determines personality.
  2. Explains attitudes of rebels, etc.
- F. Because it sets tone of life (Prov. 23:7).
  1. We determine own atmosphere.
  2. Our inner spirit determines our situation.
- G. Because life flows from it (Prov. 4:23).
  1. The things we do reveal the person we are.
  2. Christ made this very plain (Matt. 15:19; Mark 7:21-3; Luke 6:43-5).

III. How Do We Guard Our Hearts?
- A. By being careful what we allow in them.
  1. Are we as careful with our hearts as with our stomachs?
  2. Children's chorus: "Be careful little. . . ."
- B. By being careful what we allow to go on there.
  1. We do control it.
  2. We must stop what should not be.
- C. By being sure that it is right.
  1. Must be in harmony with God.
  2. "How about your heart?"

Conclusion

We have been thinking about the heart in human relationships. What is your heart in relationship to Him? He said, "My son, give me thine heart."

The Many Faces of Love
1 Corinthians 13

Introduction

"Love" is a many splendored thing." That is certainly true. The subject has as many facets as a fine diamond. Four passages of Scripture deal with the subject from a biblical perspective and form a "Biblical Valentine."

I.   **Love and Offenses (1 Cor. 13:7; 1 Peter 4:8)**
   A.   Love seeks to ignore—where it can.
      1.   Overlooks (not always looking for trouble).
      2.   Quickly forgets what has happened.
   B.   Love seeks to minimize.
      1.   Tries to make wrongs as small as possible.
      2.   Tries to deflate situations.
   C.   Love seeks to heal.
      1.   Tries to reconcile.
      2.   May involve "healing confrontation."
   D.   Love seeks to limit scope.
      1.   Tries to keep others from knowing what does not need to be known.
      2.   Rules out gossip (opposite of love).
   E.   Love seeks to do right.
      1.   Right by Biblical definition will always be what is best for individual.
      2.   Love will not be swayed from doing what is right.

II. **Love and Friction (1 Cor. 13:5)**
   "Love is not easily irritated," and most of us are. Here are some thoughts on irritation:
   A.   It is the result of the natural rub of familiarity. Things that rub against each other usually produce friction.
   B.   It is evidence of breakdown in self-control.
   C.   It is a breakdown of love.
      1.   "Love suffereth long:" endures, puts up with it.
      2.   "Love is kind:" irritation is not.
      3.   "Love vaunteth not itself:" much irritation comes from overemphasis on self.
      4.   "Love endureth all things:" even questions, stupid remarks, etc.

III. **Love and Learning (Titus 2:4)**
   Learning to love involves the following:

    A. Accepting a proper definition.
        1. As long as you accept an emotional definition, you can't learn to love.
        2. Love must be seen as more than emotions.
    B. Practicing what is taught in the Bible.
        1. Bible contains all kinds of teaching above love.
        2. We must do what the Bible tells us to do.
    C. Acting rather than waiting for feelings.
        1. Feelings follow actions.
        2. You will only feel like acting in love after you have acted in love.
    D. Looking to the example of Christ.

IV. Love and Christ (1 John 3:13-24)
    "Looking unto Jesus . . ."
    A. His love extends love to the ultimate.
        1. He has gone so far that we know everything in between is possible.
        2. This is how we know love—because He gave.
    B. His love becomes the pattern for our love.
        1. Why did Christ die?
        2. We must be thus motivated.
    C. His love should move us to action.
        1. Giving ourselves in ministry and service (Phil. 2:17).
        2. Protecting others from hazard (Rom. 16:4).
    D. His love in us tied to spiritual health.
        1. Assurance (1 John 3:19-21).
        2. Answered prayer (1 John 3:22).
        3. Fellowship with Him (1 John 3:24).
        4. Fullness of the Spirit (1 John 3:24*b*).

Conclusion
    It is good to say, "I love you." It is better to act in love. It is best to practice love in every area of life.

Hosanna!

Matthew 21:1-11

Introduction

Few stories in the Bible relate more to and are more typical of our day and age than that of the Triumphal Entry of Christ into Jerusalem. It is a hard story to understand until a few facts are in place. It is an easy story to apply when one realizes what is involved.

I.   **The Event**
   A. Two disciples sent to get donkey(s) on which to ride.
   B. Disciples throw garments on animals and assist Him in mounting.
   C. Jesus begins ride toward Jerusalem.
   D. People with Him spread garments on path and cut branches from trees.
   E. People (pilgrims) already in Jerusalem, having heard of Him, hear that He is coming, surge out to meet Him with branches, etc.
   F. The two crowds meet, enthusiasm mounts, as He nears Jerusalem the shouts of acclaim begin.
   G. Those who had witnessed the resurrection of Lazarus bear testimony and add to the enthusiasm.
   H. The Pharisees appeals to Jesus to stop the tumult (they are beside themselves with envy).
   I. Seeing the city and realizing the true nature of what is going on, Jesus breaks into weeping (based on prophetic insight as to what is going to happen).
   J. Entering the city, everyone is stirred in one way or another and people begin to ask about Him.

II. **The Explanation**
   What is going on here? What is this?
   A. Some have said it is the king's public offer of Himself as king. Interesting but quite full of problems.
   B. Actually involves several factors.
      1. Jesus promotes a showdown.
      2. Jesus is forcing the timetable of His enemies to bring things to a head in His timing (they would have preferred another time).
      3. Jesus fulfills the Messianic prophecy (people should have recognized who He was).

4. Jesus clearly reveals the issues involved.
   a. They expect a Messiah, which He is.
   b. They want a political ruler and leader.
   c. He comes as a man of peace (choice of animal).
5. Jesus secures maximum exposure for the coming week's events.

III. The Emphasis
A. No biblical story is more suited to today because so incredibly similar.
   1. Everyone is on the "band wagon" (many claim to be "born again").
   2. Great deal of public acclamation (everyone is for God and religion).
   3. Terminology is used by everyone without any common meaning or understanding.
   4. There was an intense fickleness in it all (the Hosannahs turn to "crucify him" from the same basic group of people).
   5. The whole thing was based on misunderstanding and was essentially an empty show.
B. This is so typical of today—each of these errors has its modern counterpart.
   1. This is true among the saved.
   2. This is equally true among the unsaved.

Conclusion
Do you really mean the things that you say about Christ? Do you really know the Christ that you claim to worship and hold high? If they had known what He was, they would not have shouted, but if they had known who He was they would have accepted Him just as you should.

The Way It Is

Matthew 21:1-11

Introduction

Strange how history repeats itself and basic facts don't change. So many things today are so similar to Bible times. What happened on "Palm Sunday" is being repeated over and over again today.

I. **The Situation**
   A. Background details.
      1. Festival week in Jerusalem.
      2. Jesus was staying in Bethany.
   B. The Narrative.
      1. Jesus triggers the whole thing.
      2. The fulfillment of prophecy.
      3. The reaction of the crowd.
   C. The Paradox.
      1. Multitude cries out in praise.
      2. By Friday same basic crowd is calling for crucifixion.
      3. How can we account for enormous difference?

II. **The Solution**
   Possible to suggest several things, but none of these is adequate. We rather look to the Palm Sunday crowd and four things they missed.
   A. They failed to understand who He was.
      1. They saw Him as the Prophet of Galilee (v. 11).
      2. They did not recognized Him as God's Son.
   B. They failed to understand His claims for Himself.
      1. He triggered the event, knowing the prophecy; thus He claimed to be the Savior and the Son of God.
      2. They missed the whole point of the procession.
   C. They failed to understand why He was coming.
      1. They hoped He would trigger a political revolution to break Rome's hold.
      2. There were clues present in the way He came (colt, peasants, palm branches), but they missed them.
   D. They failed to understand what He was doing.
      1. They saw a popular uprising for a peasant king.
      2. They failed to realize that He was gathering individuals unto Himself (people who really don't know what they are doing are quickly turned about in their purposes).

19

III. The Similarity

Times really don't change and we see the same today.

A. He is being generally acclaimed today.
   1. Churches are full all across the land.
   2. Acclamation is being made.

B. He is being generally misunderstood today.
   1. People don't know who He is: all sorts of opinions.
   2. People don't see what He claimed for Himself: either He is what He claimed or He is a fraud.
   3. People don't understand why He came: He came to die—no more.
   4. People fail to understand what He was doing: He still is doing it.

C. People who misunderstand are easily swayed.
   1. Explains churches that don't teach salvation.
   2. Explains "saved" who never attend.
   3. Explains your situation?

Conclusion

Men really don't change. Are you like the crowd was then?

- Hosannah on Sunday—crucify Him on Friday.
- Lord Jesus on Sunday—blasphemy on Monday.

Better get a grasp of Him before you are led astray by some force or another.

The Sight at the Cross
Matthew 27:26, 33-51

Introduction
There is an intriguing verse—36. As they sat down and watched, what did they see?

I. **The Person at the Cross**
   A. Crucifixion not distinguishing in itself.
   B. Things that distinguish this death.
      1. The refusal of sedation (v. 33).
      2. Excessive physical punishment (vv. 26, 29).
      3. Prophetic superscription (v. 37).
      4. Reaction in nature (vv. 45, 51*b*).
      5. Rending of the veil in the temple (v. 51*a*)
   C. This man identified by the very mocking of the throng—"The wrath of man praises God."
      1. A king (v. 37).
      2. A Savior (v. 42).
      3. The Son of God (43).

II. **The Event at the Cross**
   A. The culmination of history.
      1. Promise to Adam and Eve (Gen. 3:15).
      2. The calling of Abraham (Gen. 12:3).
      3. Establishment of Israel—cradle of a king.
      4. Religious symbols and rites.
      5. Prophecy (e.g. Isa. 53).
   B. The focal point of subsequent history.
   C. The dividing line in spiritual experience. In Paul, the cross becomes the center. A man's destiny is sealed by his reaction to the cross.

III. **The Victory at the Cross**
   A. Satan's claims paid.
      1. Satan had just claims.
      2. Christ paid them all.
   B. Christ's suffering ended.
   C. Man's suffering ended in Christ.
      1. No more responsible for sin.
      2. No more responsible to reach God unaided.

IV. **The People at the Cross**
   Come back to verse 36. Who were they?

A. The crowd (vv. 39, 40) mocking scorn.
B. Religious leaders (vv. 41-43) blasphemous scorn.
C. The thieves (v. 44) doubting scorn.
D. The women (v. 55) fearful devotion.
E. The Roman soldier.
   1. Before (vv. 27-31) worse than all others.
   2. After (v. 54) recognized who he was because of what they saw.

Conclusion

You have seen the people at the cross. With which group would you be identified? It may be you have never made any response before; why not take the witness of the soldiers who saw the whole thing? Accept Jesus into your heart for what He really is.

Convenient Betrayal

Mark 14:10, 11

Introduction

Modern writers and entertainers have sought to paint a "revised" picture of Judas Iscariot, but the Bible portrait stands. Take a closer look at this man and at what he did.

I.   **The Man Judas**
  A.   Describe something of his character.
  B.   One of the Twelve.
    1.   Likely Christ saw some possibility in him.
    2.   Show how often trouble rises out of the midst.
  C.   His spiritual condition.
    1.   Hotly debated.
    2.   Not of special significance.
    3.   Whether or not a believer, he could do most of what he did regardless.

II.   **What He Did**
  A.   Betrayed Christ.
    1.   Handed Him over.
    2.   Sold Him out.
    3.   Assisted His enemies.
    4.   Turned traitor.
  B.   Still being done today—betrayal of Christ common.

III.   **How He Did It**
  A.   Specific act.
    1.   More than just pointing Him out (note kiss, etc.).
    2.   Assisted hostile crowd in crucifying Him.
  B.   How it is done.
    1.   Specific denial (Peter).
    2.   Failure to defend Him when attacked (other disciples).
    3.   Failure to speak out for Him (Nicodemus).
    4.   Failure to live for Him (John Mark).
    5.   Failure to believe in Him (problem of Judas).
  C.   Whenever we go along with the hostile crowd or fail to defend Him, we betray Him.

IV.   **Why He Did It**
  A.   He had reasons (some conjecture).
    1.   Wounded feelings.
    2.   Selfishness.

          3. Ambition.
          4. Fear of consequences.
          5. Lack of commitment.
          6. Complete lack of spiritual understanding (unbelief).
      B. Our denial arises out of same reasons.

V. **The Results of the Act**
      A. The greatest condemnation ever delivered
          1. Matthew 26:5—"Friend"
          2. Luke 22:48—"With a kiss?"
          3. Acts 1:19—Public knowledge
          4. Matthew 27:3-5—Death
          5. Mark 14:21—Is it any wonder this is said?
      B. Tremendous price for betrayal
          1. For Christian: guilt, shame, rebuke
          2. For non-Christian: eternity in hell

Conclusion
    Betrayal is so convenient that we all do it all the time. The worst
form is failing to speak for Him. The most dangerous form is unbelief.
The real problem of Judas as one of unbelief. If you have never
believed, you are a betrayer of Jesus because you are agreeing with
what the devil says about Him.

Styles of Following

Luke 22:54

Introduction

The disciples at the time of the arrest, trial and crucifixion of Jesus make an interesting study. Their distribution was typical of people in His time and of people in our times as well. The disciples demonstrate three styles of following.

I.   **Those Who Turn Back and Stop Following (John 6:66)**
  A. These were followers.
    1. Who had followed Him up to this point.
    2. Who simply stopped following and turned back.
  B. They doubtlessly had their reasons for doing so.
    1. They were learning they might have to do without.
    2. They were fearful of what they might have to give up.
    3. They were afraid some things might be taken away.
    4. They were fearful of getting what they didn't really want.
  C. People today turn back for the same reasons.
    1. It is common to see people turn back.
    2. The more demanding the ministry, the more people turn back.

II. **Those Who Follow Afar Off (Luke 22:54)**
  A. Peter at the Crucifixion was typical of many throughout the ministry of Christ.
  B. These people sought an amount of distance which was comfortable.
    1. They didn't want to be too close to Him lest there be too many demands or they get in trouble over Him.
    2. They didn't want to get too close to the mob lest they be recognized as His followers and thus come under some fire.
  C. People today follow afar off for the same reasons.
    1. There is something they don't want to give up.
    2. There is something they are afraid they will lose.
    3. They are afraid of the identification with Him.
    4. They don't turn back; they just do nothing or always stay at arm's length.

III. **Those Who Couldn't Make Up Their Minds (Luke 18:28)**
  A. Peter at one time indicated that he had forsaken all to follow the Lord but later only followed Him afar off.

B. Peter's problem lay in the fact that he made the decision to follow at a good time and reneged on it at a bad time.
 1. He was faced with danger.
 2. He was faced with the demands of the unknown.
 3. He was faced with his own inadequacies.
C. Typical of many today who can't make up their minds.
 1. Follow when things are good; abandon when bad.
 2. Many follow and then drift off.

IV. **Those Who Forsook All and Followed (Mt. 16:24)**
A. John is really typical of a number of people who followed Him no matter what.
B. They were those who.
 1. Had seen there would be a cost and had counted it.
 2. Had determined that there was nothing else sufficiently worthwhile to make the cost too great for them.
 3. Had determined that the reward outweighed the price to be paid.
C. There are some like them today—may their tribe vastly increase!

Conclusion
There are several styles of following:
- Some go back and follow no more.
- Others—many others—follow afar off.
- Even others can't make up their minds.
- A few follow wholeheartedly.

What is your style of following?

If a Man Die, Will He Live Again?

Job 14:14

Introduction

Easter is time for considering the Resurrection. Even those who don't believe it do so, and all kinds of strange theories are thus propounded. Nothing is so strange as a modern use being made of the doctrine. It is being used to support the strange teaching of reincarnation.

I. **Reincarnation and Reason**
   A. Definition: The successive embodiment of the soul in a series of mortal bodies (of all kinds).
   B. Logical denial.
      1. Comes from Hinduism and Buddhism.
      2. Fails in its own purposes—no guarantee it is progressive.
      3. Does not serve cosmic justice (get punished/rewarded for deeds done in a life you are not aware of having lived).
      4. All evidence for it breaks down (beware of the demonic).
      5. It's own teaching is self-contradictory.
   C. Scriptural denial.
      1. Bible does not teach it.
      2. Bible teaches against it (Heb. 9:27).
      3. Bible never has taught it.

II. **Reincarnation and Resurrection**
   A. Different definitions: transformation of mortal body to immortal one.
   B. On-going process vs. one-time event.
   C. One form to another at random vs. lower form to higher.
   D. Vague and incomprehensible vs. clear and completely comprehendible.
   E. Self-superintending vs. superintended by the Lord.

III. **Reincarnation and Redemption**
   This is the actual contrast.
   A. Reincarnation: A means of salvation.
      1. By working one's way up through a series of reincarnations.

2. By reaching a place where delivered from such continual effort.
   3. By becoming part of some vague "eternal existence."
B. Redemption: God's means of salvation.
   1. By doing nothing except believing in what He has already done.
   2. Involves an immediate deliverance.
   3. Allows partaking of an objective eternal reality.

Conclusion

Reincarnation is another attempt on the part of man to do what God has already done for him. Man doesn't like to accept things God's way, but what is needed has already been done. What are you trusting for your eternal destiny?

The Message of the Empty Tomb

Matthew 28:1-7

Introduction

We celebrate Easter much more than "Good Friday" because the Resurrection completes the Crucifixion. It is the empty tomb that speaks to us, and it says. . . .

I.   **His Status Is Changed ("He is not here for He is risen")**
    A. He is gone from the tomb—check it out.
    B. But He is not just removed.
        1. He is risen.
        2. He is alive.
        3. He is where you can be in touch with Him.
    C. Obvious that the whole episode of death is over.

II.   **His Glory Is Revealed**
    A. His goodness is displayed.
        1. They didn't get what they wanted (the body).
        2. They got something better instead (Him).
        3. Always true for us.
    B. His promises are secure.
        1. "As He said."
        2. This was the keeping of a promise.
        3. All other promises are secure in Him including, "Lo I am with you always."
    C. His power is intact.
        1. He gave up His life (note "loud voice" on cross, John 10:17, 18).
        2. He took up His life again—He was raised, but He also arose.
        3. He says, "All power is given unto me" (thus His glory is revealed by the events of the Resurrection).

III. **His Salvation Is Assured**
    A. He defeated Satan.
        1. Resurrection was defeat of Satan's final attempt to conquer Him.
        2. He thus broke Satan's ultimate power.
    B. He disarmed him.
        1. Took away all that Satan had to use.
        2. Satan's power now is by allowance.
    C. He provided the victory for us to enjoy.

1. We share in what He accomplished.
2. Our hope lies in "riding His coat-tails."

Conclusion

The empty tomb speaks to us with a message of hope and expectation. Have you responded to that message?

- In salvation?
- In obedience?
- In living?

The Power of the Resurrection

Matthew 28:18-20

Introduction

When the women came that morning, He was gone. What would it mean if Christ had ascended directly to heaven? The disciples would never have known, and we would never know what had happened. But he remained on earth for forty days teaching, and just before He did ascend, He spoke some powerful words.

I.   **The Risen Christ Makes a Claim**— "All power is given unto me in heaven and in earth" (v. 18*b*)
   A. Nature—all power is His.
      1. Authority and control.
      2. Hard to describe but Paul attempts it (Col. 1:15-19; Phil. 2:9-11).
   B. Its extent.
      1. "All"—whole realm of known things.
      2. Only limit is His voluntary self-limitation (Heb. 2:8).
   C. Source.
      1. He can say it because He rose.
      2. If He had stayed dead, all other power lost.
      3. Because He rose, He can say, "all" power is given to Me.

II. **The Risen Christ Gives Some Commandments**— "Go ye therefore and teach all nations, baptizing them in the name of the Father and of the Son and of the Holy Ghost, teaching them to observe all things whatsoever I have commanded you" (v. 19).
   A. Details.
      1. Given to all believers, not just disciples.
      2. Activity is commanded.
      3. Our trouble today is passivity.
   B. Contents.
      1. Disciple all nations (through preaching Gospel).
      2. "Baptize them."
      3. "Teaching them to observe."
         a. Not Old Testaments commandments.
         b. His commandments as He gave them and the New Testament develops them.
   C. Basis.
      1. "Therefore" because of this.

2. Commandments based on claim.
   a. Claim gives Him right to command.
   b. Claim means He has power to enable.
3. He commands in the power of the resurrection.

III. The Risen Christ Makes a Covenant
A. Basis.
   1. Made by the risen Christ—only way it could be true.
   2. Goes with other two.
B. Its extension.
   1. "Always"—"everyday."
   2. "Unto the end of the world"—"Unto consummation of age."
C. Its meaning.
   1. Risen Christ with His own.
      a. Not visible but knowable.
      b. In salvation and service.
   2. This makes keeping of commandments possible.

IV. The Evangelistic Application
A. Let's consider His authority.
   1. He had "all."
   2. What is your relationship to it?
B. Let's consider His commandments.
   1. Commanded His disciples three things.
   2. You are disobedient and in defiance of His authority until these things are done.
   3. Discipleship most important.
   4. Are you a disciple or a defiant?
C. Let's consider His promise.
   1. Who is it for?
      a. Those who recognize His authority.
      b. Those who have been obedient to His will.
   2. What does it mean?
      a. Perfect peace within as we yield to Him.
      b. Absolute assurance.
   3. Can you say, "Lo, He is with me always?" He wants you to be able to say it.

Conclusion
The power of the resurrection is tremendous. You either know it in your heart or resist it in your heart. Easter would be a wonderful time to stop resisting and start knowing.

What's New?

2 Corinthians 5:17

Introduction

We ask many insincere questions of others, and "What's new?" is a common one. When that question is asked regarding spiritual things, however, it has some striking answers.

I. **We Have a New Hope**
   A. Mark of the unconverted is being without hope.
   B. Christianity gives us hope.
      1. For this life in answered prayer.
      2. For eternity in assurance of heaven.

II. **We Have New Feelings**
   A. Unconverted tend to be ruled by passions.
      1. So often do what they don't mean to do.
      2. Actually under the dominion of Satan.
   B. We have ability to rule passions (if we will).
      1. We are not forced to do things in emotional realm.
      2. We have freedom from domination.
      3. We have new emotions like peace, freedom from guilt, etc.

III. **We Have a New Purpose/Direction**
   A. We formerly had one of two purposes.
      1. Go for what we had decided we wanted.
      2. Follow the direction of the devil.
   B. Now we have a new direction and purpose.
      1. The will of God becomes the big issue in life.
      2. We have the Word of God to show us the will of God.

IV. **We Have a New Destiny**
   A. The unconverted heading for Christless eternity.
   B. We have the destiny of eternity in heaven.

V. **We Have a New Understanding**
   A. For the unconverted, the Bible is a closed book.
      1. He can read it, but he can't understand it.
      2. The end result is that he misses so much truth and accepts so much error.
   B. The child of God has his eyes opened to Scripture.
      1. He can read and understand what it says.
      2. Thus he has a much greater understanding of the world around him which is clearly interpreted in the Bible.

VI. We Have a New Potential

A. Two people of equal ability have vastly different potential.
  1. Does not mean they will achieve differently.
  2. One of the tragedies is that Christians do not live up to potential.
B. Differences.
  1. "The fear of the Lord is . . . wisdom" (Ps. 111:10).
  2. "The fear of the Lord is . . . knowledge" (Prov. 1:7).
  3. Understanding of Scripture which saves so much time and effort.
  4. Inner help of the Holy Spirit.
  5. Advantage of answered prayer.

VII. We Have a New Attitude

A. As a result of all this, we should have a new and different attitude.
  1. We should not apologize or retreat.
  2. We should never view Christianity as a burden.
B. Degree to which we are willing to accept both the blessings and claims of Christ is the degree to which we will have a new attitude.

Conclusion
What's new?

When the Day Was Come
Acts 2:1-4

Introduction
Pentecost stands out as one of the most significant, exciting, new, dramatic, dynamic days in the history of the church. The Spirit of God came, was given, became present, and here's what happened.

I. **Everone Knew About It**
    A. "Was noised abroad."
        1. Sound.
        2. Reports of events.
    B. Whole city knew.
        1. Vast multitude.
        2. Crowded for feast.
    C. Explanation of large churches. When the Spirit of God is really present, everyone knows it!

II. **New Things Began to Happen**
    A. Outward manifestations.
        1. Sound like rushing wind.
        2. Tongues like fire.
    B. Spread of Gospel.
        1. Only Palestine to this point.
        2. Spread begins right here.
        3. Corresponds with Genesis 10 and 11.
    C. Church begins.
        1. New Testament sense.
        2. Start of new economy of God. When the Spirit is really present, new things begin to happen.

III. **People Did Things Previously Impossible**
    A. Broke out of wait into action.
        1. Not possible before.
        2. This is why they were to wait.
    B. People spoke with other tongues.
        1. All were filled and all spoke.
        2. Obviously foreign languages.
        3. Symbol of tongue. When the Spirit of God is present, people begin to do things previously impossible.

IV. **People Were Changed**
    A. They had understanding.

1. "Straitened" previously.
2. Knew more in one day than ever before (Peter's sermon).
   B. They had character changes (Luke 24:19-21).
      1. They did not lose faith but did lose hope. Hope was restored.
      2. They lost courage (Peter). Courage was restored. When the Spirit really is present, people are changed.

V. Things Were in Accord With the Bible
   A. Nothing here out of harmony with Word.
      1. Fulfills prediction.
      2. Results in biblical preaching.
   B. Special tie in with Old Testament.
      1. Most feasts have New Testament correspondence.
      2. "Day of Pentecost was being fulfilled."
   C. Spirit and Word must agree.
      1. Spirit active in writing of Word.
      2. God cannot contradict Himself. When the Spirit is really present, things will happen in full accord with the Bible.

IV. Souls Were Saved
   A. This was harvest festival.
   B. Harvest granted.
      1. 3,000 saved.
      2. Continual results.
   C. Spirit's presence always does this.
      1. Revival issues in evangelism.
      2. Deeper things involve evangelism.
      3. Evangelism at heart of God. When the Spirit is really present, souls are saved.

Conclusion
There are the exciting things that happen when the Spirit is present. Is His presence felt in your life? Are you blocking His presence in the church? Have you ever received Christ to know His presence in the first place?

God Said, "I Love You"

Acts 1:11

Introduction

Christ arose from the dead and stayed on earth for forty days, clearly establishing the fact of His resurrection. He ministered to His disciples during this time by giving commands, providing information, and asking questions. At the end of that time He was bodily taken up into heaven in the ascension.

I. **The Ascension Marked the End of His Earthly Ministry**
    A. Had completed what He came to do.
        1. Everything that had happened was according to plan.
        2. The plan was now completed.
    B. Now time to depart.
        1. No need for continued breach in fellowship.
        2. Prepared the way for the coming of the Spirit.

II. **The Ascension Marked the Beginning of Heavenly Phase**
    A. Present at the presence of the Father.
        1. Went back from whence He had come.
        2. Acts 2:33; Hebrews 8:1.
    B. At Father's right hand.
        1. Not physical place.
        2. Term for authority and preference.

III. **The Ascension Began a Specific Program of Operations**
    A. He is exercising universal authority (Col. 1:16, 17).
    B. He is asserting headship in the church (Col. 1:18).
    C. He is bestowing spiritual gifts (Eph. 4:8).
    D. He is serving as advocate (pleads the blood on behalf of the saints) (1 John 1:8).
    E. He is the intercessor (prays for His own) (Heb. 7:24).
    F. He is building the celestial city for His saints in the future (John 6).

IV. **The Ascension Gave a Specific Promise**
    A. His return.
        1. He stated it frequently.
        2. The angels confirmed it.
    B. Gave specific details.
        1. In air.
        2. Literal physical.

3. Without announcement.
4. Connected with His saints.

V. **The Ascension Began His Working Toward a Specific Purpose**
   A. Clearly stated (Heb. 2:10).
      1. To bring many sons to glory.
      2. To see many take steps which will lead to glory.
   B. Secondary.
      1. To provide eternal keeping (Heb. 7:25).
      2. To provide them all they need for living the godly life.
      3. To keep His people form the dominion of Satan.
   C. Purpose demands individual participation.
      1. Man has so much provided for him.
      2. He must accept what God has provided.

Conclusion

He ascended up on high, and He did so for you. Have you recognized this fact and acted on it?

In God We Trust

Zechariah 4:6

Introduction

America has a rich Christian heritage, even our coins speak of our trust in God. But she seems to have fallen on hard times lately, and there are many who continuously remind us of that fact.

I. **The Condition of America**
   A. Society becomes more and more depraved (Abortion, no-fault divorce, living together, crime, pornography, immorality, cheating).
   B. Politics has become something of a wasteland.
      1. Elected officials do not keep their promises.
      2. Leaders seem to have no sense of morality.
      3. The courts become more and more centers of tragi-comedy.
   C. And the church in general has problems.
      1. Lack of Christian impact. We supposedly have more Christians than we have ever had, but we surely have less influence than ever.
      2. Lack of biblical Christianity. The average Christian is in no way different from the average good person.
      3. The condition of our youth is appalling. Our Christian kids are often little different from the world.
      4. The condition of our churches is unreal. They are often little more than religious social clubs.

II. **The Things That Won't Help**
   A. Movements will not get the job done even though we have more than ever before.
      1. Mass evangelism.
      2. Political involvement.
      3. Moral movements.
      4. Revival ministries.
      5. Constitutional amendments.
   B. None of these failures should amaze us as God has already indicated how He normally works in Zechariah 4:6.

III. **What Can An Individual Do?**
   A. Individuals can do far more than we like to think.
      1. Witness Gideon.
      2. Note Deuteronomy 20:5-9.

B. Specifics.
   1. Prayer.
   2. Personal participation in society.
   3. Raising children with biblical values.
   4. Winning the lost.
   5. Supporting churches that stand for that which could turn things around.

Conclusion

There is something tangible that you and I can do. What are you doing along these lines?

Great Days!!

1 Thessalonians 4:13-18

Introduction
Many special occasions in the life of the church. We may question the appropriateness of some celebrations, but God has had—and will have—some great days according to Scripture.

I. **The Concept of Great Days**
    A. The Bible has clusters of the miraculous.
        1. At the Creation.
        2. At the time of the Exodus.
        3. At the time of the prophets.
        4. At the day of Pentecost and the founding of the church.
    B. God has also had His great days.
        1. Creation.
        2. The Covenant day at Sinai.
        3. The dedication of the Temple.
        4. Incarnation day.
        5. Crucifixion day.
        6. Resurrection day.
        7. Ascension day.
    C. But some of God's greatest days are yet to come.

II. **The Description of Days to Come**
    A. The Rapture of the church (1 Thess. 4:13-18).
        1. The next great event.
        2. Describe what will happen.
        3. Absolutely nothing necessary beforehand.
        4. Great differentiator.
    B. The Second Coming (Rev. 19:11-16).
        1. Distinct from the Rapture (discuss intervening events).
        2. Actually coming of Christ to earth with His people.
        3. The beginning of a 1,000 year reign of truth.
    C. The Judgment.
        1. The "bema"—judgment seat of Christians (1 Cor. 5:10).
            a. Not according to sin.
            b. According to what we have done with what we have been given.
        2. The "Great White Throne" judgment (Rev. 20:11-15).
            a. The judgment of sinners for failure to accept God's provision.
            b. The final, inescapable judgment.

III. The Import of These Great Days

    A. All are sure and yet to come.
1. All are described in a Bible that is always proved true.
2. All have not as yet happened.

    B. Not everyone will participate in all.
1. Some people will participate in the Rapture, Second Coming and Judgment Seat of Christ.
2. Others will participate in the "Great White Throne" but not in any of the other things.

    C. The difference in the future big days is being made in the present.
1. Decisions now determine destiny then.
2. You are deciding right now what you will do and where you will be in eternity.

Conclusion

We ought to use the special day we have to be sure we are ready for the great day to come. This is a special day. You could make it more so for yourself by preparing for the days to come on this day.

A Godly Mother

Proverbs 31:10-31

Introduction

The portrait of a godly woman painted by Lemuel in this passage is both priceless and timeless. Surely the expression of God's unchanging will, this portrait provides a pattern for female emulation.

I. **Her Sphere**
   A. Marriage.
      1. The pattern woman is married.
      2. Marriage not required, but certainly not wrong.
   B. The work of the home.
      1. Primary responsibility.
      2. Does not rule out employment.

II. **Her Character**
   A. Trustworthy.
      1. She is faithful.
      2. She is sympathetic.
      3. She is intelligent.
   B. Provident.
      1. She makes provision for the future.
      2. She looks to the welfare of her household.
   C. Industrious.
      1. She was involved in business affairs.
      2. Appears always busy.
   D. Strong.
      1. Physical strength necessary for all listed duties.
      2. Spiritual strength needed for impact on family.
   E. Loving.
      1. She has concern for the poor.
      2. She is a "need meeter."
   F. Gracious.
      1. "In her tongue is the law of kindness."
      2. Her speech brings peace to her household.
   G. Spiritual.
      1. She "feareth the Lord."
      2. This is the basis of all other qualities.

III. **Her Reward**
   A. In her influence.
      1. She influences her family.
      2. She influences others as well.

B. In her successes.
1. What she does, prospers.
2. The prosperity of her home depends on her.
C. In her family.
1. Her family hold her in honor.
2. The greatest honor comes from those who know us best.
D. In her continuing influence.

Conclusion

The pattern provided by this woman is a big one to model, but it is one attainable by a woman who will order her life in obedience to the Word of God.

Our Father: His Character
Luke 11:1-4

Introduction

The Lord's prayer is full of teaching. Simply reading it petitions reveals many things about what God is really like. There are actually eight characteristics of God mentioned in the brief scope of the prayer.

I. **God Is a Personal God— "Our Father"**
    A. Speaks in terms of relationship and fellowship.
    B. Only people can enjoy those factors with others.
    C. He is more than a force; He is a person to whom we are related.

II. **He Is a Preeminent God— "Which art in heaven"**
    A. His location in heaven shows the exaltation of His person.
    B. He is the only contact we have in heaven.
    C. He ought to be superior to any other person and ought to enjoy a more preeminent place than any other person or thing in our lives.

III. **He Is a Praiseworthy God— "Hallowed be thy name"**
    A. May thy name be highly lifted up and exalted.
    B. This is primarily done two ways.
       1. By our expressions of praise.
       2. By our lives.

IV. **He Is a Promising God— "Thy kingdom come."**
    A. He has promised His kingdom on earth.
    B. The prayer is for it to come relative to time not relative to whether or not it will happen.
    C. "All the promises of God in Him are yea and amen."

V. **He Is a Powerful God— "Thy will be done on earth as it is in heaven"**
    A. This is not an empty prayer.
    B. His will is already being perfectly done in heaven.
    C. He can—and will—also do His will perfectly on earth at the Word of His power.

VI. **He Is a Providing God— "Give us this day our daily bread"**
    A. Give us our "day by day" bread (the amount we need for each day).

B.   He has promised to meet our needs but gives us so much more.

VII. **He Is a Pardoning God**— "And forgive us our debts as we forgiven our debtors"
A.   He readily and completely forgives us.
B.   He does so as we forgive others so that we might not develop into hypocrites.
C.   "To err is human; to forgive divine."

VIII. **He Is a Protecting God**— "And lead us not into temptation but deliver us from evil"
A.   He is able to protect us.
B.   We must call upon Him for that protection (a lot of our problems come from not praying about this).

Conclusion

What a God! Is your God as big as this God? Do you know what it is to be forgiven by God?

Obedience to Parents
Ephesians 6:1, 2

Introduction

A most unpopular subject—this matter of obedience to parents. Most feel no need of a message on the subject, and some just plain don't like it. A message heeded now may avoid pain later.

I. **Commandment: Children, obey your parents**
   A. Absolutely commanded in clear terms.
   B. Obedience must be proper.
      1. Complete.
      2. Immediate.
      3. Cheerful.

II. **Considerations: Why should I obey my parents?**
   A. Because it is right.
      1. God said so.
      2. It is right according to the order God established.
   B. Because parents know more.
      1. May seem incredible.
      2. Have been around at least twice as long as you.
   C. Because God wants you to learn submission to authority.
      1. Very important character trait.
      2. Spiritual significance.
         a. If you won't submit to the parents you see, how can you submit to the God you can't see?
         b. If you can't submit to parents, how to husband or employer?
   D. Because of love.
      1. Your parents, except in unusual cases, love you.
      2. You should love your parents.
         a. Just for what you owe them.
         b. Should show in what you do and say.

III. **Conditions**
   A. In all things?
      1. Only condition is where their command would violate a clear command of God.
      2. Everything else is covered.
   B. What about "poor" parents?
      1. Your responsibility is to do what God says to do.
      2. You are responsible for you.
      3. Your parents' poor performance is no excuse.

IV. **Cautions**
    A. This is the only way to happiness and blessing.
        1. If God says to do it, we must do it.
        2. God blesses obedience.
        3. Failure is to ask for problems.
    B. The sowing and reaping principle.
        1. What you put in, you get back.
        2. Pertains in this realm also.
    C. The potential danger to life.
        1. "That thou mayest live long on the earth."
        2. Two possible interpretations.
            a. Obedience will keep you out of danger.
            b. God may punish disobedience.

Conclusion

The Bible commands obedience to parents, and any other way is out of His will and thus potentially dangerous. You need to set your heart to obey no matter what. It is the only way to blessing.

Come Home, It's Suppertime

Luke 22:19, 20

Introduction

Much controversy flares around who is eligible to partake of the Lord's Supper. We don't want to bar the way; we want to open the door as widely as possible in harmony with the Word. Careful examination of the actual institution of the supper will give us clear teaching concerning how widely the door can be opened.

I. **Teaching From the Meaning of the Ordinance**
    A. Note the statements of Christ (Luke 22:19, 20).
        1. "This is my body broken for you."
        2. "This is my blood shed for you."
        3. "This do in remembrance of me."
    B. It is a memorial of the death of Christ.
        1. Something akin to a holiday.
        2. Proper observance requires understanding of its meaning.
    C. The Lord's Supper is open to those who understand the meaning of His death.
        1. The only way to properly understand it is to have received Jesus as your Savior.
        2. For someone to partake who has not done this is both a travesty and a blasphemy.

II. **Teaching From the Symbolism of the Ordinance**
    A. Note the symbolism involved.
        1. Just breaking bread and pouring out wine would adequately symbolize truth in His death.
        2. Goes one step further and tells them to eat.
    B. Meaning.
        1. Symbolizes partaking of Him.
        2. Christ is to the soul what bread and wine are to the body.
            a. That which nourishes.
            b. That which sustains life.
            c. That which satisfies hunger.
        3. We are to feed upon Him; that involves.
            a. Fellowship.
            b. Obedience.
    C. The Lord's Supper is open to those who are in feeding and obeying fellowship with Christ.

III. **Truth From the Situation of the Ordinance**
    A. There is an interesting stress on unity and oneness in the account.

1. They were all together in one place.
2. The object lesson of footwashing was designed to teach this.
3. They all ate and drank.
   B. There is a specific commandment given along this line (John 13:33-35).
   1. They were commanded to love one another.
   2. There were two reasons for the command.
      a. The obvious one: so that all men might know by it that they were His disciples.
      b. The less obvious one: connected with His going in verse 33, they were going to need to stand together because He was leaving them.
   3. They did stay together in response to His commands.
   4. We speak much of the success of the early church; this was in a measure due to their obedience to this specific command.
   C. The Lord's Supper is open to those who are in fellowship with one another in the Lord.

IV. **Truth in an Accompanying Incident (John 13:2-17)**
   A. Christ's washing of the disciples' feet.
   1. Did so because of their failure to do so.
   2. Did so also with a mind to instruct.
   B. Sought to teach two things in the incident.
   1. The need for humility and mutual service.
   2. The need for continual cleansing for the child of God.
   C. The Lord's Supper is for those who are clean from sin.
   1. Process of cleansing begins with exposure to Word.
   2. It is carried out through confession.

V. **Truth in the Reaction of the Disciples (Mark 14:17-21)**
   A. Christ intimated betrayal quite clearly.
   1. Didn't identify who it would be or how.
   2. Raised some questions in the minds of the disciples.
   B. Disciples' reaction interesting.
   1. Each one knew he was in the clear, as far as intent was concerned, but each wanted to be sure of himself.
   2. The degree of our willingness to examine ourselves is usually the measure of our need for it.
   C. The Lord's Supper is for those who have passed through self-examination concerning these other matters (1 Cor. 16:28-32).

Conclusion

Our purpose is not to block from the communion table, but rather to invite to it all who are ready. If you are not, why not get ready now?

Communion Meditation

1 Corinthians 11:23-34

Introduction
    Why do you take Communion? You should have a good answer to this. The answer lies in the basic meaning of Communion.

I.   **An Opportunity for Careful Self-Examination**
    A.   Scripturally stated: "Let a man examine himself."
    B.   Urgently needed.
        1.   Because of the business of the day.
        2.   Because of natural tendency to gloss over sin.

II.   **A Specific Art of Worship**
    A.   The nature of worship: declaring the worth and wonder of God.
    B.   The way in which communion is worship.
        1.   Opportunity for meditation.
        2.   Time of prayer and praise.

III.   **A Constant Reminder of Certain Spiritual Truths**
    A.   Reminds us of the death of Christ.
        1.   Main design of the ordinance.
        2.   Death particularly as related to atonement.
    B.   Reminds us of some facts about His death.
        1.   The extent of His death: for all.
        2.   The availability of His death: freely offered.
        3.   The appropriation of His death: individual must take.
    C.   Reminds us that we must feed on Christ for sustenance.
        1.   Vital concept and neglected area.
        2.   Symbolic.
    D.   Reminds us of the fact of communion.
        1.   Does not primarily signify our communion with other Christians.
        2.   Has primary reference to communion with God and Christ.

IV.   **An Encouragement to Evangelism**
    A.   Speaks of this throughout.
        1.   Extent of His death.
        2.   Availability of His death.
        3.   Appropriation of His death.

B. Specific reference: "Show forth His death."
  1. An active demonstration.
  2. For the purpose of inducing others to take part.

Conclusion

Why do you take Communion? Hopefully you now have good reasons for doing so.

Check-Point Charlie

1 Corinthians 11:31

Introduction
During the days of a physically divided Berlin, Germany, there was a notable place—called "Checkpoint Charlie"—where everyone and everything were checked. Checkpoints are helpful in life, and commencement is one of those checkpoints.

I. **What You Should Check**
    Are you on course?
    A. Scholastically: grades, knowledge.
    B. Socially: maturity, cycles of life.
    C. Spiritually : are you what you claim to be?

II. **How You Should Check It (2 Cor. 10:12)**
    A. Should not judge by ourselves.
    B. Should not judge by others.
    C. Should judge by Word. Two criteria only valid standard.
        1. God's expectations.
            a. Have to do with ability.
            b. Are you the best that you could be?
        2. God's commandments.
            a. Have to do with obedience.
            b. Are you doing what you should do?

III. **What You Should Do About the Check**
    A. Confess wrong.
    B. Commit to change.
    C. Commence action.
    D. Challenge self-progress.

Conclusion
Some are committing themselves to mediocrity. Some are committing themselves to problems. Some are committing sins of unreality. Why not stop at the checkpoint?

A Text for Labor Day
Proverbs 23:4

Introduction

A man who was about to be baptized placed his wallet in a plastic bag. The minister said, "That's not necessary." The man said, "Oh, yes it is." He understood what Martin Luther meant when he said that a man must have two conversions, one for his soul and one for his pocketbook.

I.   **The Commandment**
    A. Does not say, "Labor not."
       1. Labor is part of man's natural state.
       2. Labor is not result of fall—fall only makes harder.
    B. Does say, "I labor not for riches."
       1. Takes away riches as motive.
       2. Deals with real purpose of labor.

II. **Reasons for the Commandment**
    A. Riches are temporal (1 Tim. 6:7).
    B. Riches are transitory (Prov. 23:5*b*).
    C. Riches are teasing (Prov. 27:20; Eccl. 5:10).
    D. Riches are tranquilizing (Matt. 13:22; Rev. 3:17).
    E. Whole matter summarized by 1 Timothy 6:17.

III. **Alternatives**
    A. Really understand God (Jer. 9:23, 24).
    B. Be rich toward God (Luke 12:16-21).
    C. Lay up treasure in heaven (Matt. 6:19-24).
       1. Meet needs of others (Prov. 19:17).
       2. Spread Word of God.
       3. Meet needs of God's work.

Conclusion

Someone once likened giving to throwing money in a hole. A better analogy is putting it in the pneumatic tube at the bank. It disappears, but it goes somewhere. Labor not to be rich unless it is to be rich in treasure laid up in store.

How Can I Say Thanks?

Ephesians 5:20

Introduction

Thanksgiving is a reminder to be grateful and the Bible says much about gratitude. How can I say "thanks" at this season?

I. **By Giving Thanks**
    A. Grateful acknowledgment of blessings.
    B. Involves recognizing and accepting blessings.

II. **By Giving Thanks Always**
    A. Pray without ceasing; thank without ceasing.
    B. Covers every situation.
        1. After situation is over.
        2. During situation (Jonah 2:1, 9; Paul in prison).
        3. Before situation on basis of promises.

III. **By Giving Thanks in All Things**
    A. Covers things which appear bad or good.
        1. Good things are easy to be grateful for.
        2. Bad things are hard to be grateful for.
    B. Covers things both withheld and given.
    C. Need to be looking for new things (creative thanks).

IV. **By Giving Thanks to God**
    A. The source of everything.
        1. Direct source of good.
        2. Indirect source of evil.
    B. Gratitude to Him should make us grateful to others.

V. **By Giving Thanks in the Name of the Lord Jesus**
    A. Recognizing His place in all we have.
    B. Recognizing that without Him we have nothing.
    C. Recognizing all spiritual blessings come from Him.
        1. Things worth thanking for.
        2. Real blessings: salvation, spiritual life.

Conclusion

That is how to say "thanks," but why should we say thanks? Thankful living eases burdens, lifts spirits, eliminates self-pity, focuses on what God may be doing for us in difficult situations, enlarges our concept of God, and increases our faith. Do you live thankfully? Can you thank Him for the greatest gift, eternal life?

Thanksgiving as a Thermometer
1 Chronicles 16:4; 23:30; 29:13

Introduction
Praise is an expression for what God is; thanks is an expression for what He has done. They are different, but they go together. Just as our temperature reveals what's going on inside, so our thanks and praise serve as a thermometer of our spiritual state.

I. **They Reveal the Degree to Which Circumstances Control Our Lives**
A. Can't change many circumstances.
B. Can control response to them.
C. See them as allowed of God and respond properly.

II. **They Reveal the Degree to Which We Are Self-centered and Selfish**
A. Far more selfishness than obvious.
B. Selfish interpret everything in term of how it affects them.
C. Thanks and praise show that focus is off self.

III. **They Reveal the Degree to Which Joy Dominates Our Lives**
A. "A deep joy is the reward of a thankful spirit."
B. "Unthankful person never joyous" (for long).
C. Thanks and praise reveal a system where joy can dwell.

IV. **They Reveal the Degree to Which We Are Submitted to His Will**
A. We know Romans 8:28; we just don't always accept it.
B. We often think we know better.
C. Thanks and praise—no matter what—reveal a spirit that accepts what God sends and that is submitted to His will.

V. **They Reveal the Degree to Which We Understand What Life Is All About**
A. Life is merely prelude to eternity.
B. Those things count most in life which contribute most to eternity.
C. Many of the things we count most important will matter the least in eternity.
D. Thanks and praise show our understanding by paying Him what we owe.

Conclusion
Just as a thermometer tells about your physical health, so your spirit can tell about your spiritual health. How are you at thanks and praise? How are you at the things they reveal? What are you going to do about it?

A Journey of Faith

Luke 1:39-45

Introduction

There are several trips associated with the birth of Christ. The first was when Mary went to see Elizabeth. After receiving the message from the Lord, Mary was likely very confused and went seeking someone to confide in etc.

I. **The Challenge of Faith**
    A. Zacharias greatly challenged (vv. 13-17).
        1. He knew (or should have known) what was involved.
        2. Involved great difficulty (v. 18).
    B. Mary greatly challenged (vv. 28-38).
        1. Given much detail.
        2. May not have understood much.
        3. Involved human impossibility.

II. **The Contrast of Faith**
    A. Both asked questions (vv. 18, 34).
        1. Reactions to them very different.
        2. Difference must be in questions.
            a. Zacharias: How can something like this be?
            b. Mary: How are you going to do this?
    B. Significant differences.
        1. Zacharias was older; should have known better.
        2. Zacharias faced less impossible promise.
        3. Zacharias was spiritual leader.

III. **The Certainty of Faith**
    A. Promises will come to pass (v. 45).
        1. This is absolute certitude.
        2. Statement here is always true.
    B. Person always has option—belief or unbelief—can chose to be Zacharias or Mary.
        1. Many go through life dumb with unbelief.
        2. Others face life like Mary.
            a. Went perplexed; came rejoicing.
            b. Went for comfort; came with assurance.
        3. Difference is simple matter of faith.
            a. What He promises, He can do.
            b. What He has said, He will do.

Conclusion

The incredible challenge of Christmas is that God will do what He has promised. "Difficult" and "impossible" are unknown to Him. We have the choice of Zacharias or Mary as our pattern. What is the impossible He has promised you in His Word? Will you be a Zacharias or a Mary?

How Far Is It to Bethlehem?

Luke 2:1-7

Introduction

The prophet had said that Messiah would be born in Bethlehem, but Joseph and Mary didn't live there. This "advent adventure" got them to Bethlehem.

I. **It Was a Difficult Journey**
  A. Especially hard for Mary.
    1. Pregnancy situation.
    2. Customs of day would make things more difficult.
  B. Almost everything in connection with Christ was difficult for her (2:35).
    1. Surroundings of His birth.
    2. Everything recorded in life.
    3. Even tender word on cross.
  C. We expect nothing difficult in connection with Him (and where there is something difficult, we turn back).

II. **It Was a Designed Journey**
  A. Planned by Roman government.
    1. It was a census leading to taxation.
    2. Note Joseph's submission to government.
    3. If he did as some today, Christ would not have been born in Bethlehem.
  B. Over all was the plan of God.
    1. It was the "fullness of time."
    2. All accomplished by Augustus Caesar.
    3. God over-rules. Who remembers much about Gaius Julius Caesar Octavius Augustus?
  C. Reveals true nature of ultimate power.
    1. Traveling because God on throne.
    2. Remember God still works in world today.

III. **It Was Demonstrative**
  A. Note Bethlehem.
    1. It was fulfillment of prophecy.
    2. Why the prophecy?
      a. Historic significance: Rachel, Ruth, David, Samuel.
      b. Deeply connected with David.
  B. Note the housing.
    1. No room and what a room.

      2. Deepest possible humiliation.
      3. Intensely predictive of His life and death.
   C. Note the whole situation.
      1. Rejected.
      2. Humbled.
      3. Lowest elements of society.
      4. Gentile presence (wise man).
      5. "But as many as received Him. . . ."

Conclusion

There are three messages to be heard in this journey:

- God controls human affairs.
- There is a price for "giving Him birth."
- "Have you any room for Jesus?"

The Ultimate Journey
John 1:12, 14

Introduction
This is the ultimate journey ever made by anyone. It is the journey of Christ from heaven to earth. Two verses tell us volumes about the trip.

I. **It Was a Painful Journey**
   A. Note the changes involved.
      1. Locations: glory to gory.
      2. Form: freedom to limitations.
      3. Context: adoration to mockery.
      4. Status: uncontested to contradicted.
      5. Time zones: eternal to temporal.
   B. Difficult to illustrate.

II. **It Was a Purposeful Journey** (He made the journey and endured the changes for certain specific reasons.)
   A. He came to do the Father's will (Lk. 2:49; John 4:34, 5:50, 6:38; Mt. 26).
   B. He came to minister to people (Mt. 10:28).
   C. He came to give His life a ransom (Mark 10:45).
   D. He came to give mankind abundant life (John 10:10).
   E. He "endured the cross, despising the shame," to fulfill them His commitment to His purposes.

III. **It Was a Powerful Journey** (He was able to accomplish what he purposed.)
   A. He gave the right to become sons of God.
      1. Obvious that all were not such.
      2. "Power" means right.
      3. All the things that go with sonship.
   B. He gave it to those who did something.
      1. Received Him/believed on His name.
      2. Terms explain each other.
   C. He gave it to "as many as."
      1. Open to all.
      2. Open only to those who respond.

Conclusion
The ultimate journey involved the ultimate price, purposes and power. What does it mean to you personally?

Wise Men From the East
Matthew 2:1-12

Introduction
 All of the journeys that were made that first Christmas involved some difficulty, and this one was no exception. It is an interesting story and the subject of many traditions.

I.   **Who They Were**
   A. Who they were not.
      1. Know little about them.
      2. Greek church traditions source of confusion.
   B. Who they really were.
      1. Stargazers.
      2. From Greece/Persia.
   C. How they knew.
      1. Great tradition in world of that day.
      2. There were likely Jews where they were.

II. **What They Showed**
   A. Great commitment.
      1. Journey very great.
      2. Difficulties very significant.
      3. Realities very uncertain.
   B. Great contrast.
      1. They knew: Jews had to check.
      2. They came: Jews didn't.
      3. They followed through: Jews were totally apathetic.
   C. Great consecration.
      1. Their worship of king.
      2. Unwittingly worshiped the Savior.
      3. Brought homage. Likely financed trip into Egypt.

III. **Why They Came**
   A. Show universal impact of His coming.
   B. Show indifference of His people.
   C. Show true nature of His life/ministry.
   D. Show providential care of Father's treasure.
   E. Show significance of His person.

Conclusion
 These Magi from the East were much wiser than modern man. Most men fail to heed signs or make any effort to find Him. Even His own people fail to worship Him. Are you a wise man?

CHRISTMAS (Advent Adventures V)

The Flight to Egypt
Matthew 2:13-23

Introduction

The last advent journey reveals a strange chapter in life of our Lord. It also reveals much about God's operation and provides a splendid New Year's consideration.

I. **God Knows the Unknown**
   A. Much that Joseph didn't know.
      1. Likely course of wise men.
      2. Plans of Herod.
      3. Anything about Egypt.
      4. Death of Herod.
      5. "Where" of return.
      6. Reign of Archalaeus.
      7. Return to Nazareth.
   B. God knew all these things and moved in accord with them.
   C. He knows all about our unknowns and moves in accord with that knowledge.

II. **He Cares tor the Uncared For**
   A. Humanly speaking, no one cared for the royal family.
      1. No one looking after them.
      2. Unknown in Egypt.
   B. God provided abundantly.
      1. Gold, frankincense, myrrh.
      2. Carpentry in Egypt.
      3. Jews to help Jews.
   C. God provides specially for those who have no one to care for them (fatherless and widows).

III. **He Controls the Uncontrolled**
   A. Herod, a man out of control.
      1. The character of the man.
      2. The conduct of the man (no problem with the slaughter given his nature).
      3. The control of the man.
         a. God caused his death.
         b. Tragic ironies in death.
   B. God controlled the man and his ability to harm His Anointed.

C. Uncertainties of new year must be seen in light of control of God.

IV. **He Reveals the Hidden**
   A. Gives Joseph information.
      1. Uses medium of dreams.
      2. Gives only as much detail as necessary.
      3. Note Joseph's complete obedience.
   B. God always gives necessary information.
   C. We have a more sure word of prophecy.
      1. Would like to have direct revelation.
      2. Actually written record is much more beneficial.
      3. What makes us think we would obey direct revelation when we don't obey written?

Conclusion

God did all this for His child, but you are His child as well, or are you?